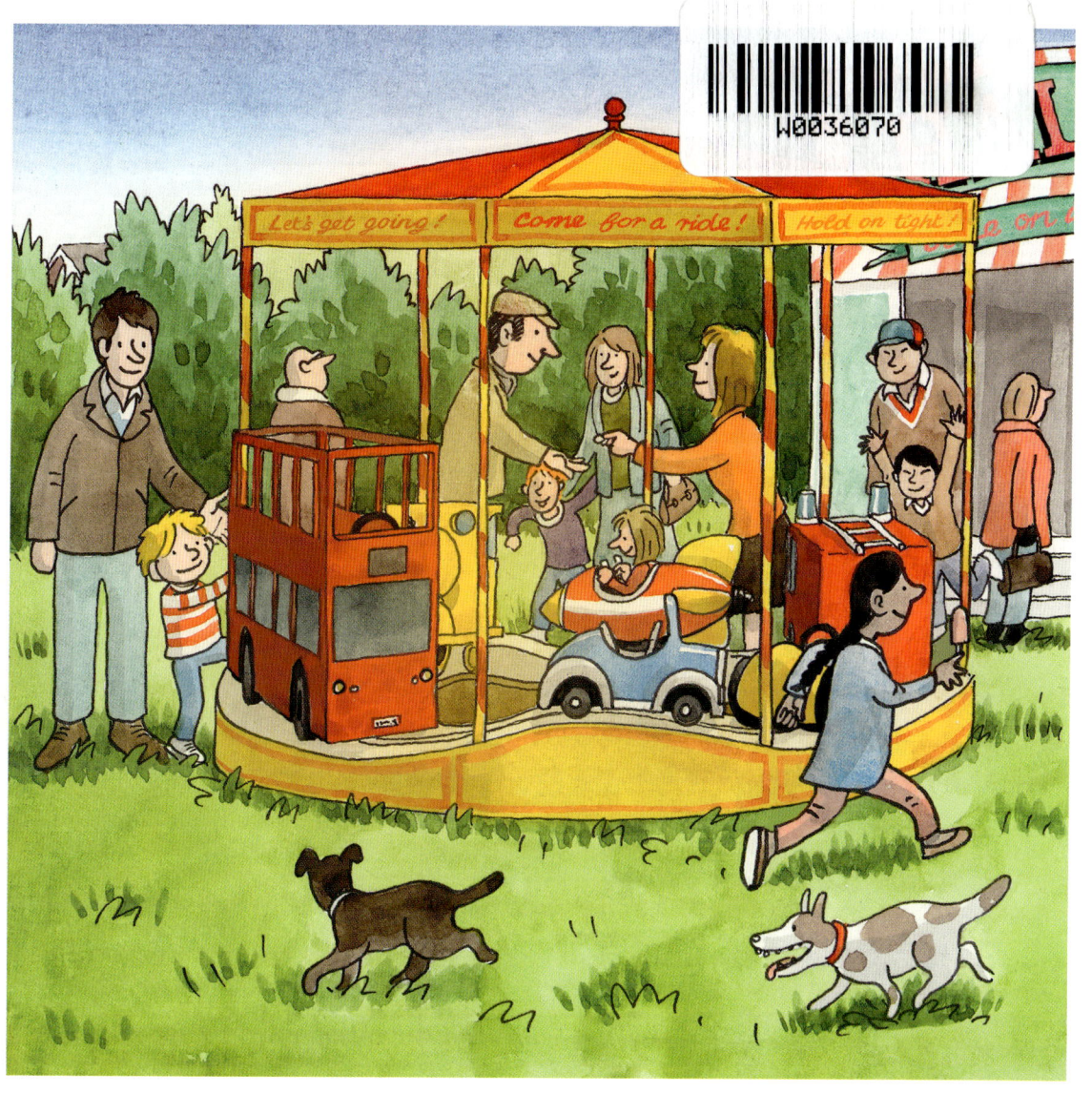

Kipper got on the bus.

W0036070

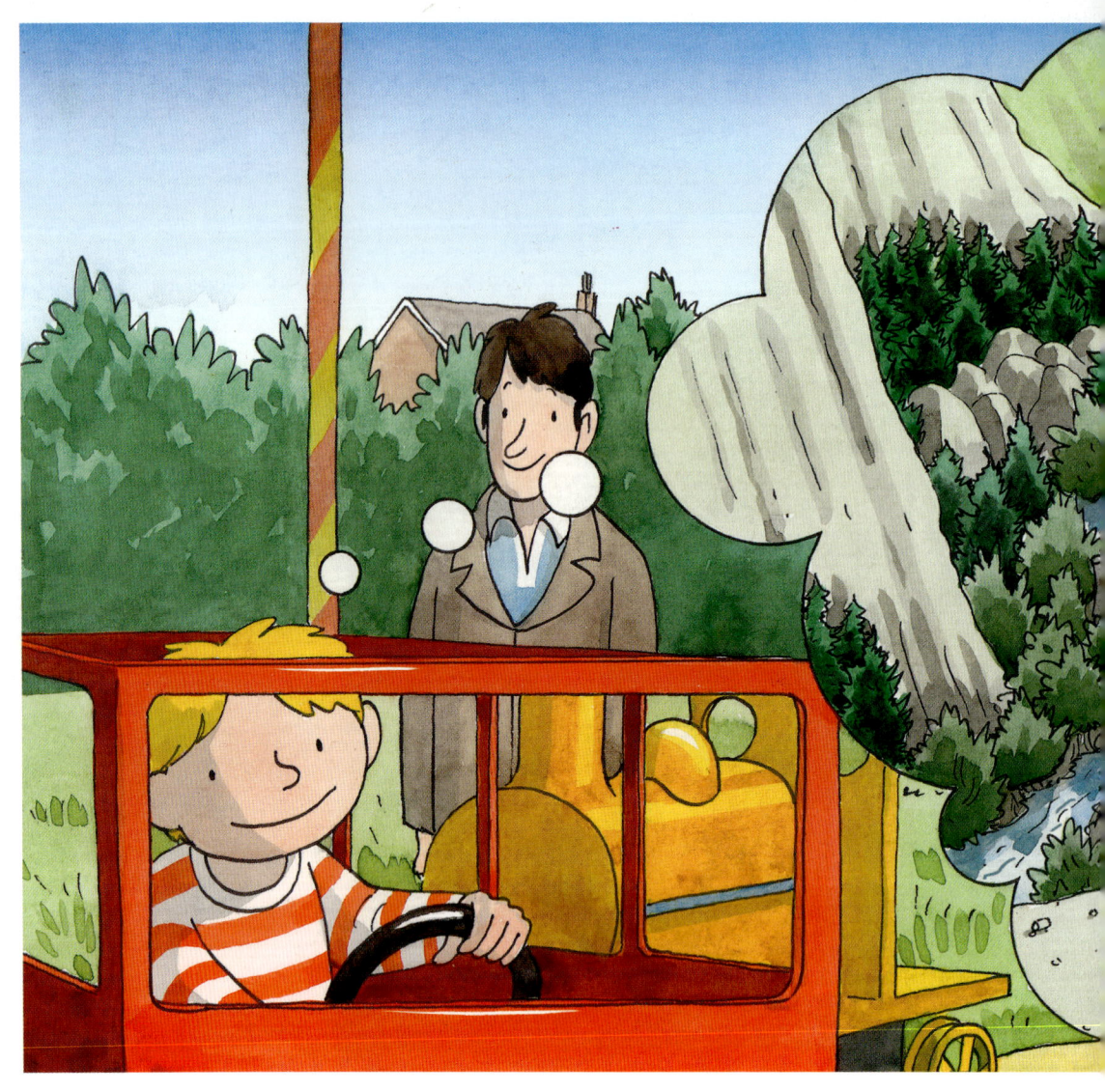

It was the big, red bus.

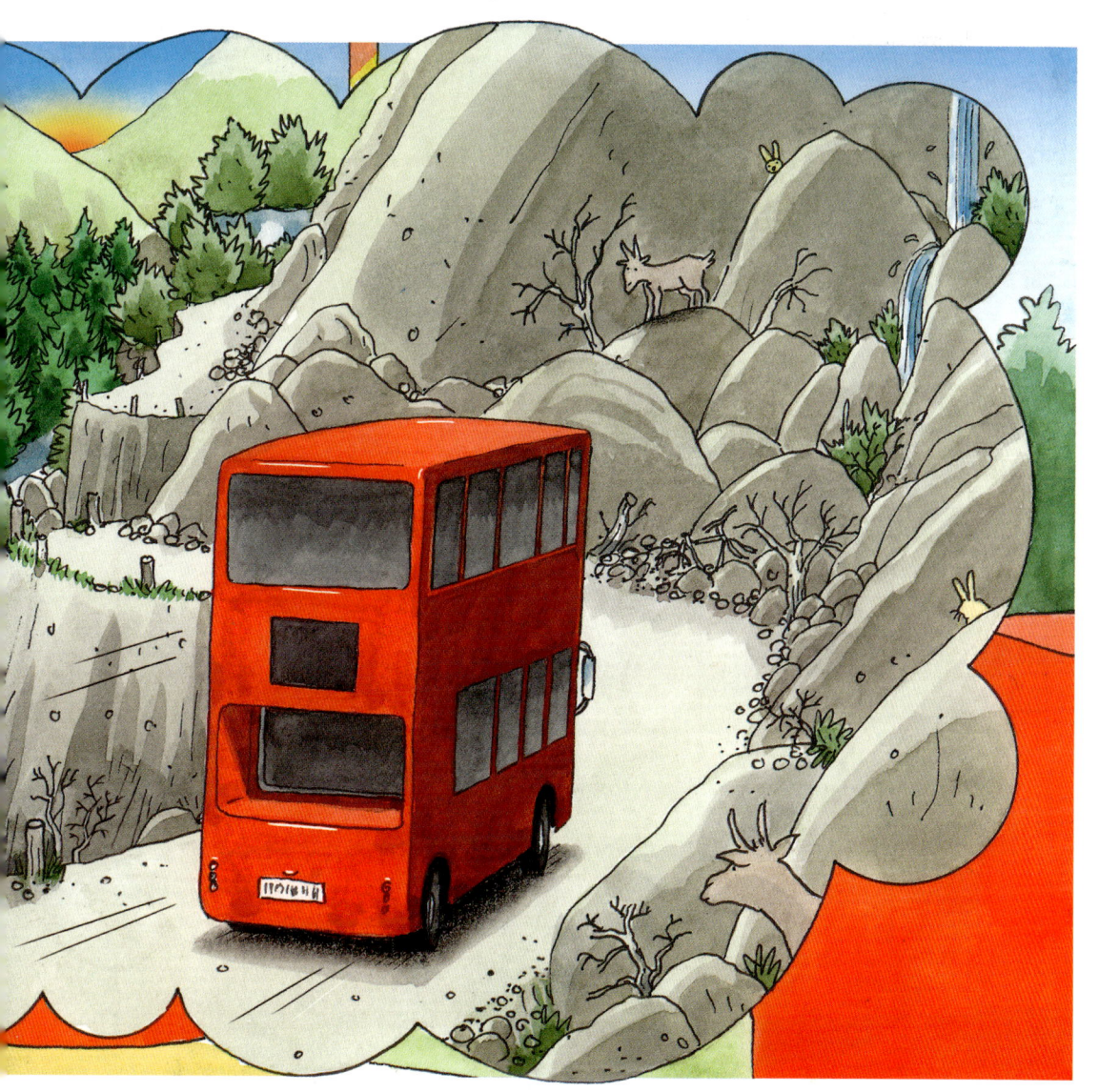

The big, red bus set off.

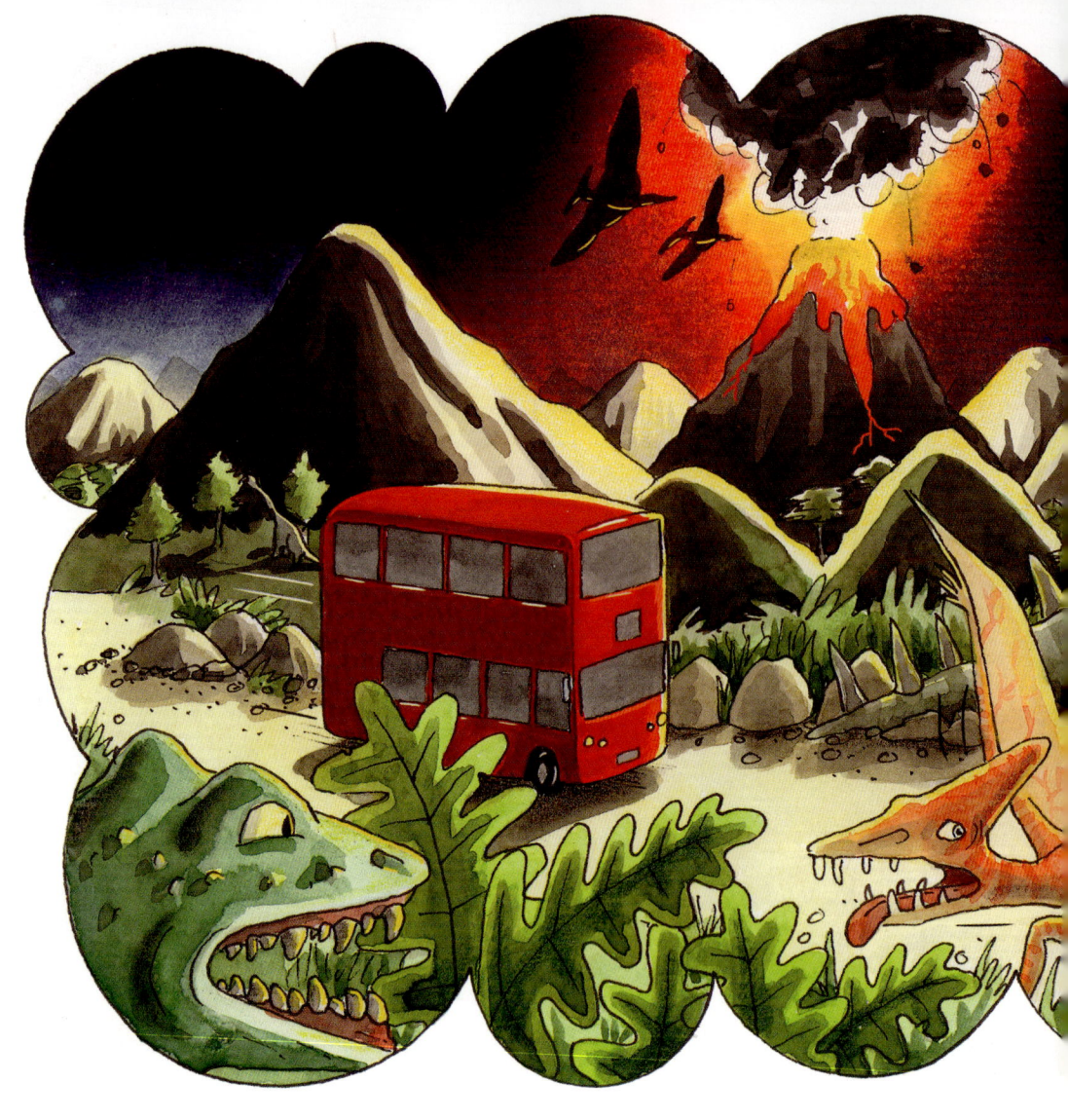

He went to Dinosaur Land.

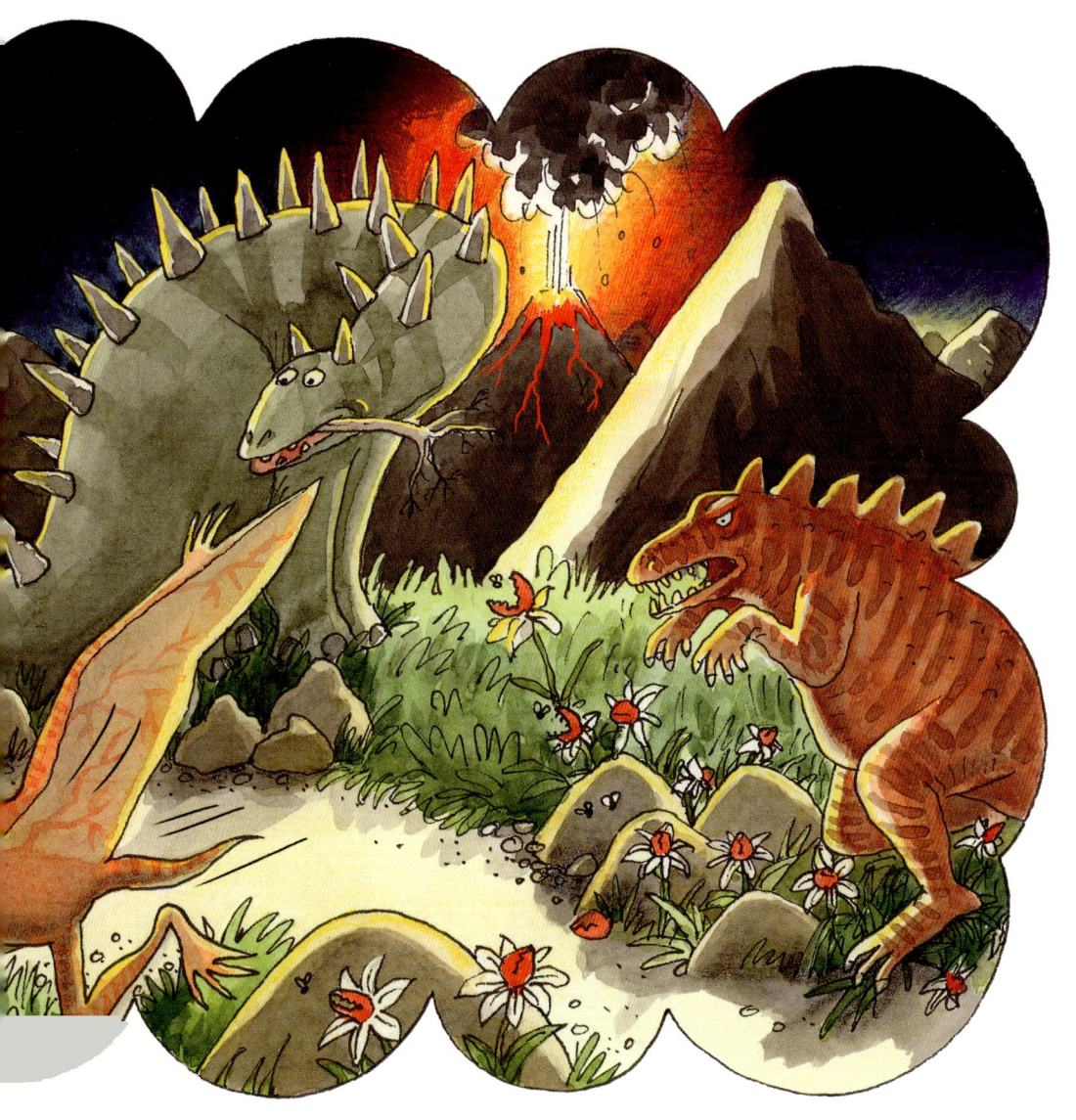

It had a lot of dinosaurs.

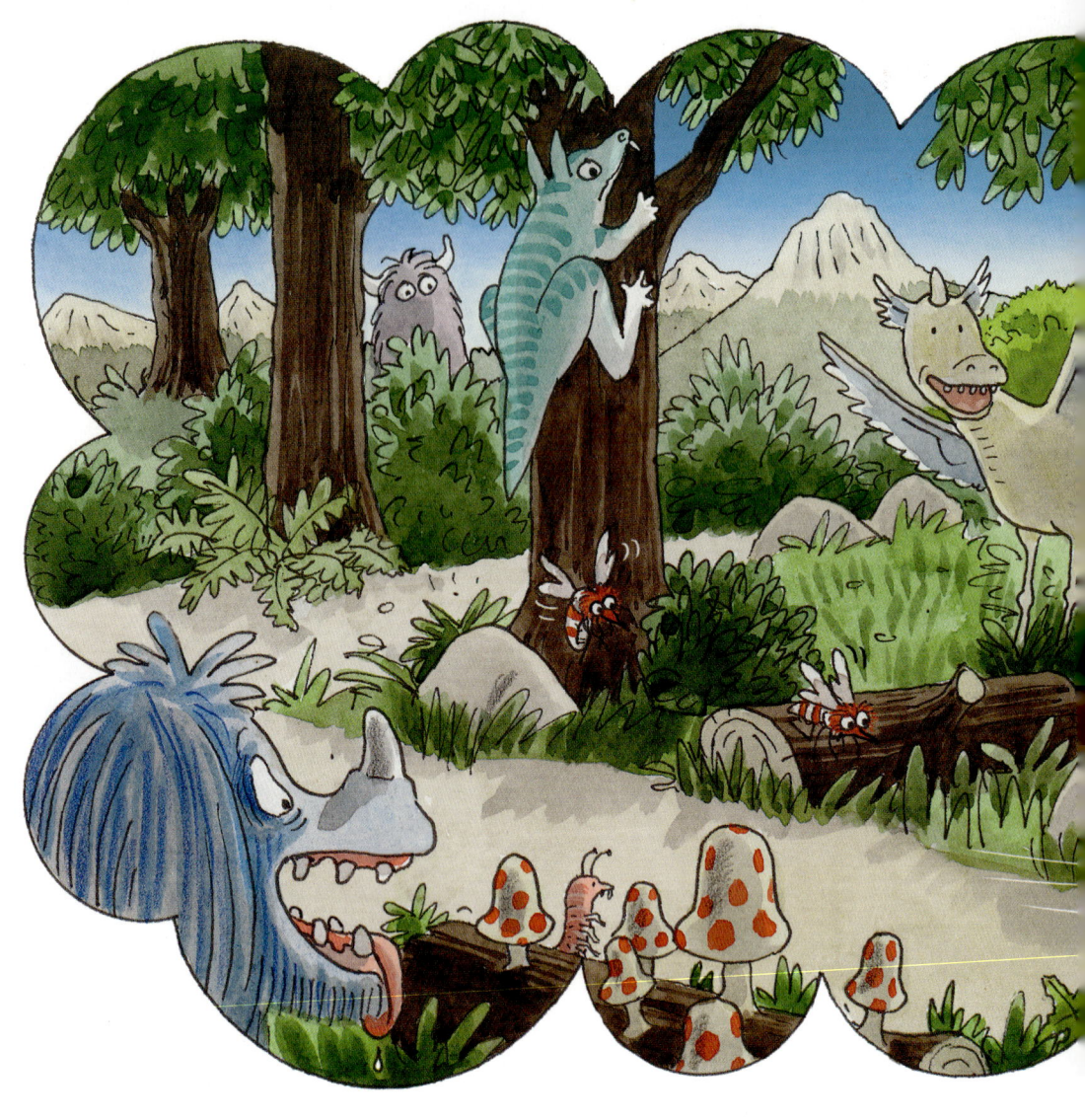

He went to Monster Land.

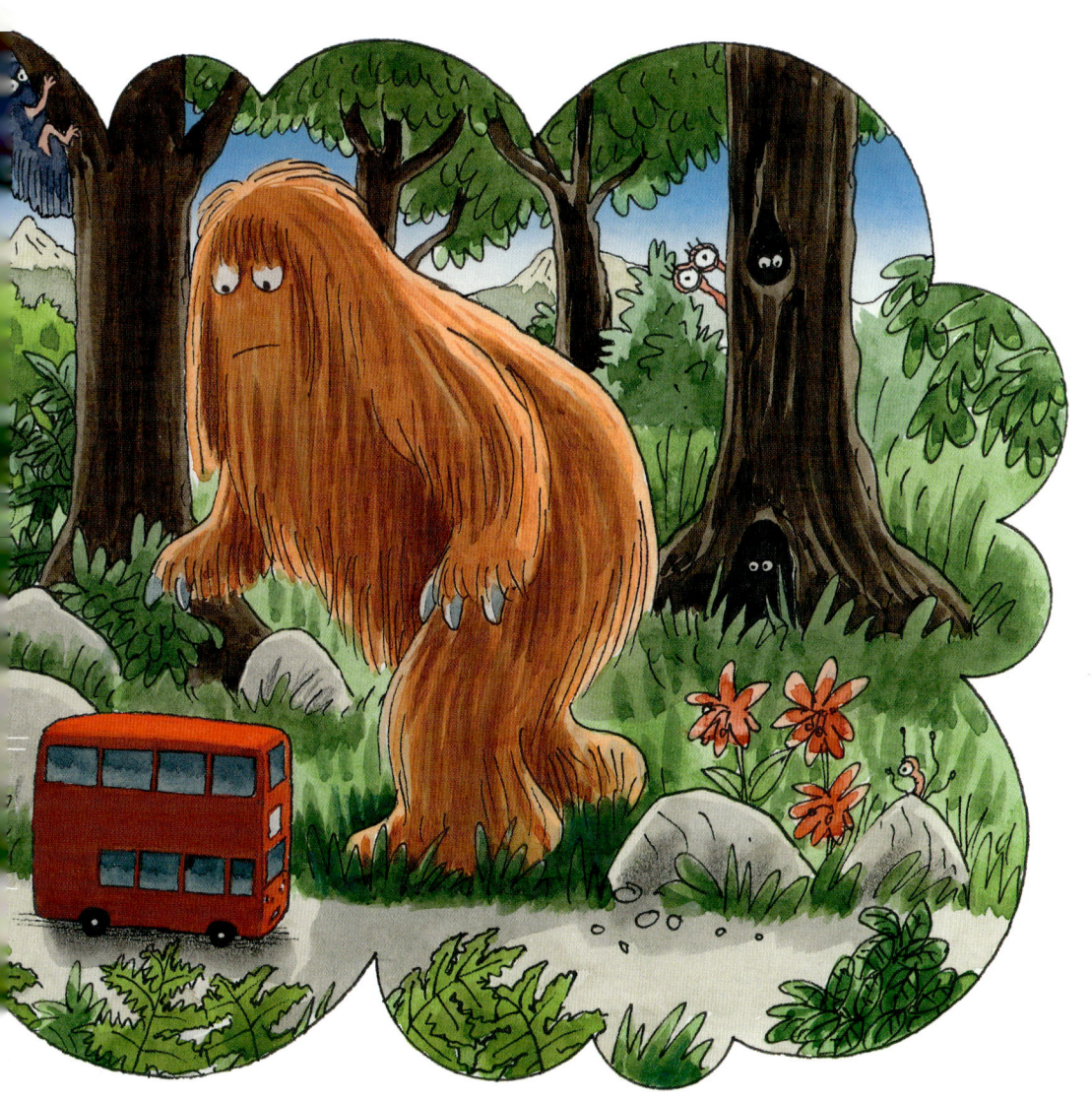

It had a lot of monsters.

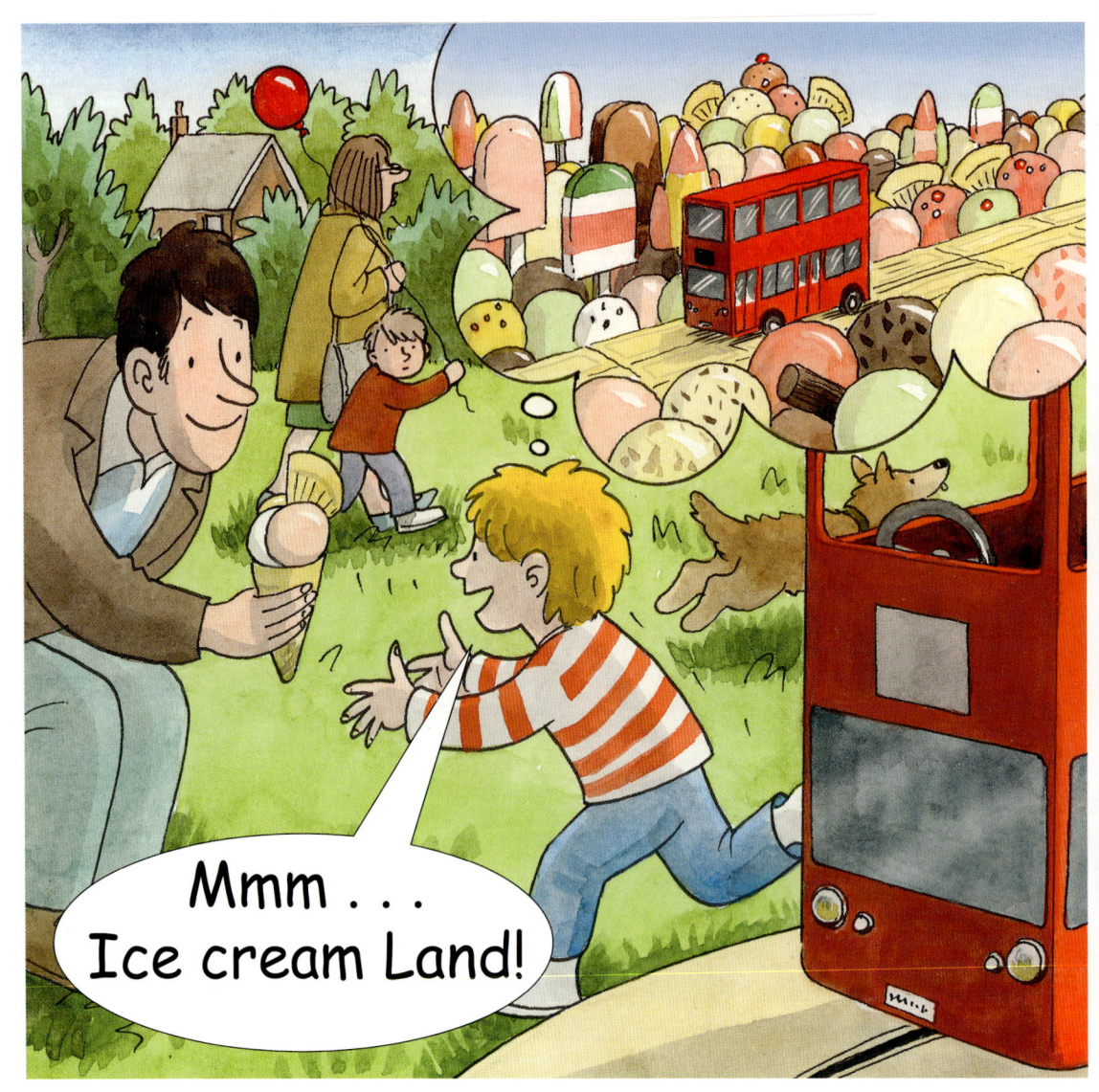

Kipper got off the bus.